SHAKESPEARE
MADE EASY
King Lear

Tanya Grosz & Linda Wendler, Ph.D.

WALCH PUBLISHING

The classroom teacher may reproduce materials in this book for classroom use only.
The reproduction of any part for an entire school or school system is strictly prohibited.
No part of this publication may be transmitted, stored, or recorded in any form
without written permission from the publisher.

1 2 3 4 5 6 7 8 9 10

ISBN 0-8251-4994-0

Copyright © 2004
Walch Publishing
P.O. Box 658 • Portland, Maine 04104-0658
walch.com

Printed in the United States of America

Contents

To the Teacher v

Introduction to the Play vi

Introduction to Shakespeare xvii

    Activity 1: Honesty Versus Flattery (Act one, Scene 1) 1

    Activity 2: Deception Everywhere (Act one) 2

    Activity 3: Goneril and Regan Deal with Dad (Act one, Scenes 3–5) .. 3

    Activity 4: The Jester Who Told the Truth (Act one, Scene 4) 4

    Activity 5: Review 5

    Activity 6: Shakespearean Insults (Act two, Scene 2) 6

    Activity 7: Poor Edgar (Act two, Scene 3) 7

    Activity 8: The King Breaks Down (Act two, Scene 4) 8

    Activity 9: Courtly Reporter (Acts one and two) 9

    Activity 10: Review 10

    Activity 11: Civil War in Britain? (Act three, Scene 1) 11

    Activity 12: Predictions (Act three) 12

    Activity 13: Words of Wisdom from a "Madman" (Act three, Scene 6) . 13

    Activity 14: Event Recall (Act three) 14

    Activity 15: Review 16

    Activity 16: Father and Son Reunion (Act four, Scene 1) 17

    Activity 17: Answered Letter (Act four, Scene 2) 18

    Activity 18: A Marriage Gone Bad (Act four, Scene 2) 19

    Activity 19: The Letter Informing Cordelia of All (Act four, Scene 3) .. 20

    Activity 20: Review 21

    Activity 21: Nature of Man Questionnaire 23

    Activity 22: A Portrait of Three Sisters (Act four, Scene 3) 24

    Activity 23: Wisdom in Insanity (Act four, Scene 6) 25

    Activity 24: Headlining (Act four) 26

Activity 25: Review 27
Activity 26: Values Profile 28
Activity 27: Spying on Edmund (Act five, Scene 1) 29
Activity 28: Reviewing the Deaths 30
Activity 29: Writing an Obituary 31
Activity 30: Review 32

King Lear Final Test 33

Culminating Activity 1: Nature and the Nature of Man 35
Culminating Activity 2: Create a Movie Poster or a Book Jacket 36
Culminating Activity 3: *King Lear* and Current Events 37
Culminating Activity 4: Put It to Music 38
Culminating Activity 5: Write Your Own Ending 39

Answer Key 40

To the Teacher

As any teacher or student who has read Shakespeare knows, his plays are not easy. They are thought-provoking and complex texts that abound with romance, deceit, tragedy, comedy, revenge, and humanity shown at its very worst as well as its very best. In short, to read Shakespeare is to explore the depths and heights of humanity.

The *Shakespeare Made Easy* Activity Guides are designed by teachers for teachers to help students navigate this journey. Each guide is broken into six sections of four activities and one review. At the end of each guide is a final test, a variety of culminating activities, and an answer key. The activities are meant to aid textual comprehension, to provide creative opportunities for the reader to make personal connections with the text, and to help busy teachers gain quick access to classroom-tested and age-appropriate activities that make the teaching of Shakespeare an easier task.

Each regular activity, as well as each culminating activity, can be modified to be an individual or a group task, and the reviews and tests can be used as quick comprehension checks or formally scored assessments. The guides may be used in conjunction with the Barron's *Shakespeare Made Easy* texts or alone. Ultimately, the *Shakespeare Made Easy* Activity Guides are intended to assist teachers and students in gaining an increased understanding of and appreciation for the reading of Shakespeare.

Introduction to the Play

Background to *King Lear*

King Lear begins in the same way as many fairy tales do: "Once upon a time, there was a great king who had three daughters. The two older daughters were ugly and mean, but the youngest daughter was beautiful and kind." Shakespeare takes this story, however, and turns it into one of the most moving, horrifying, and despairing tragedies of the English language.

Shakespeare's play follows an old Celtic legend about King Leir. He wishes to retire in comfort and so plans to disperse his kingdom among his three daughters, but he expects to keep his title and his knights. Before doing so in a royal ceremony, he asks each daughter to state how much she loves him. The two older daughters use flowery language to express their love and devotion to King Leir. The youngest daughter, Cordeilla, makes a simple statement. Infuriated, the King disinherits Cordeilla, and she moves to France to marry the French king.

King Leir visits his oldest daughter, Gonorilla, with sixty of his knights, but it is too much work for her, and she demands that he keep only thirty knights. Leir is angry and goes to his middle daughter Regan. She, however, says he can only have five knights if he stays with her. Leir, humbled, goes back to Gonorilla but is now told he can only have one knight. Leir travels to France and is reunited with Cordeilla and the French king. They gather an army and return to England, successfully overthrowing the rule of the two older daughters and their husbands. Leir retakes the throne and rules successfully for three years. At his death, Cordeilla rules for five more years. When her nephews come of age, however, they mount a rebellion against Cordeilla and are victorious. She is put in prison, where she kills herself.

Shakespeare's *King Lear,* while reuniting King Lear and Cordelia, ends not with King Lear on his throne, but with betrayal, suffering, madness, and death.

In addition, *King Lear* is enhanced with a subplot. This part of the play involves the Earl of Gloucester and his two sons, Edmund and Edgar. For this part of the play, Shakespeare adapted a story from Sir Philip Sidney's *Arcadia* in which a king is betrayed by his illegitimate son and mistakenly exiles his true son. The true and forgiving son protects the father, who is blind, from falling off a cliff.

The two plots are linked by the common element of a father who misjudges and disinherits the true child. The father favors the false child, who seeks to destroy the father. Ultimately, the father is "saved" by the true child. When the father understands the mistake and the pride that led to his downfall, the reader sympathizes with the father and is agonized by the price the father has to pay to attain this new awareness. Also, in each story, the child readily forgives the father and is reunited with him. This level of forgiveness and restoration is truly amazing and inspiring.

Introduction to the Play

Synopsis of *King Lear*

Act one, Scene 1

The Earl of Kent and the Earl of Gloucester discuss how King Lear will divide the kingdom. Gloucester introduces Edmund as his illegitimate son. Although he is a bit ashamed that he had a son out of wedlock, Gloucester acknowledges Edmund to be his son.

King Lear enters. He announces that he will divide his kingdom in order to prevent any problems. His plan is to retain the name of king and keep a retinue of one hundred knights, but to leave matters of government to his sons-in-law. He wishes to give the best third of the kingdom to the daughter who loves him the most. He invites Goneril, his eldest daughter, to express her love first. She uses very flowery language to express her love, and King Lear gives her a third of the kingdom. Cordelia, in an aside, implies that Goneril's formal declaration is insincere. Regan speaks next and tries to exceed Goneril's language. She pleases King Lear, and he gives her another third of the kingdom. He then asks Cordelia to state her love. She replies to King Lear's command by saying, "Nothing." King Lear is enraged at her failure to express her love to his satisfaction, and he disinherits Cordelia and splits the kingdom in two between Goneril and Regan. The Earl of Kent tries to persuade Lear to reconsider his actions, but King Lear will not listen to Kent's wise advice. In fact, Lear banishes Kent.

Without a dowry, Cordelia is offered as a bride to both the Duke of Burgundy and the King of France. Because she is now poor, Burgundy rejects Cordelia, but the King of France is happy to marry her. Cordelia then says goodbye to her sisters and instructs them to take good care of their father. After she leaves, the two older sisters comment that if Lear can turn so quickly against Cordelia, he can certainly turn against them. They agree to keep tight control of their father.

Act one, Scene 2

Edmund speaks a soliloquy in which he expresses his disgust at how he has been treated because he is illegitimate. He feels he should be seen as equal to his legitimate brother, Edgar. The Earl of Gloucester enters, confused about the disarray in the kingdom due to Lear's hasty decisions. Edmund pretends to be putting away a letter in order to get Gloucester to ask him about it. Gloucester reads a phony letter that suggests Edgar is plotting to kill Gloucester to inherit all his money and lands. Edmund pretends to caution Gloucester against a rash decision, and he says he will have a conversation with Edgar that Gloucester can overhear in order to determine if Edgar is indeed planning to murder his father. Gloucester wonders at all the disorder in the world.

After Gloucester leaves, Edmund expresses his scorn at those who think that the stars control people's lives. He then meets Edgar and tells him that his father suspects him of villainy. Edgar leaves in dismay that his father would think he was disloyal.

Introduction to the Play

Act one, Scene 3

Goneril complains to her steward Oswald that caring for King Lear and all his knights is a tremendous burden. Lear is irritable, and the knights are always partying. She tells Oswald to feel free to be rude to Lear so that he might move on to Regan's castle.

Act one, Scene 4

At Goneril's castle, Kent, in a disguise and with a country accent, offers his service to King Lear, who accepts Kent's offer. Goneril's servants insult King Lear and his knight. The Fool enters and teases Kent for offering to be a servant to King Lear. He also hints that King Lear is a fool to give all his power and possessions to his two daughters. He tells Lear that he has cut an egg in the middle and given away the inside to his daughters, leaving only an eggshell—an empty crown for King Lear.

Goneril enters and expresses her displeasure at the behavior of Lear's one hundred knights. She demands that he reduce the number of knights in his charge by half, since he does not need them anymore. Lear is extremely angry, and he denies the charge that his knights are unruly. He curses Goneril's womb so that she will never have a child, or if she does, her child will betray her as Goneril has betrayed Lear. He also realizes that Cordelia was a truer daughter than Goneril. Goneril's husband, Albany, comes in and is amazed at all the disorder around him.

After Lear exits, Goneril instructs Oswald to send a letter to Regan to warn her that Lear is coming and what has happened.

Act one, Scene 5

The Fool talks with Lear, saying that he "should not have been old until he had been wise." Giving away all his power has put him at the mercy of his two daughters.

Act two, Scene 1

Edmund tricks Edgar into fighting with him. Gloucester enters to see his two sons with their swords out, and he is convinced that Edgar is indeed planning to murder him. Edmund reports that Edgar is not worried if Edmund tells of his brother's evil plans, because no one would believe him since he is an "unpossessing bastard." Gloucester, fully under the influence of Edmund's lies, promises Edmund that he will try to improve his status.

The Duke of Cornwall and his wife Regan enter. Gloucester informs them of Edmund's loyalty and protection. Cornwall is impressed with Edmund's "virtue and obedience" and asks him to serve in his court.

Act two, Scene 2

Oswald and Kent meet, and Kent calls Oswald a knave and a rascal. Kent challenges Oswald to fight because Oswald carries letters against King Lear. Kent begins to beat Oswald. During the beating, Edmund, Cornwall, Regan, and Gloucester enter. They discover why Kent is beating Oswald. As punishment, Kent is placed

Introduction to the Play

in the stocks for the entire night. Gloucester pleads with Cornwall and Regan not to put Kent into the stocks because King Lear will take it as an insult. They refuse and leave. Gloucester apologizes to Kent for his situation, but Kent tells Gloucester not to worry; he will sleep the time away.

Act two, Scene 3

Edgar, in a soliloquy, announces that he will play the part of a poor beggar in order to escape from being hunted by his father and Edmund.

Act two, Scene 4

Lear and the Fool find Kent in the stocks. When Lear realizes that his daughter has done this, King Lear feels he is almost suffocating from hysteria, and he leaves. The Fool teases Kent for being in the stocks. King Lear returns with Gloucester and, in a fit of passion, tells Gloucester to inform Cornwall and Regan that he will speak to them about their actions.

Regan and Cornwall enter, and King Lear tells them how vilely Goneril has treated him. Regan replies that Lear should go back to Goneril and ask for her forgiveness. Lear is amazed at this, and he curses Goneril that she might become lame and blind. Then, his fury building, he asks who put his servant in the stocks. Goneril enters and joins hands with Regan, who encourages Lear to return to Goneril with fifty men. Lear refuses and states he will stay with Regan, keeping his one hundred knights. But Regan replies that Lear can only bring twenty-five men to her castle. Lear quickly turns back to Goneril to take up her offer of fifty knights. Goneril then states that Lear does not need any retinue at all. Lear, in despair, feels he will go mad at their demeaning actions, and exits with Gloucester, Kent, and his Fool.

Gloucester returns to say that the King is highly angry and is looking for a horse to ride away. Goneril, Regan, and Cornwall are hardened against King Lear's plight and decide to lock the doors against him, even though a wild storm is coming.

Act three, Scene 1

Kent speaks to a Gentleman, who says that King Lear is out in the storm with only the Fool. Kent informs him that there is division between Albany and Cornwall, and that France may be using this weakness to attempt a takeover. He then asks the Gentleman to give a ring to Cordelia and tell her what is happening to her father.

Act three, Scene 2

Lear is exposed to the storm and commands it to rage and blow even more. The Fool, however, wishes for some shelter. Kent, still in disguise, enters and tells King Lear and the Fool about a hovel. Lear expresses sympathy for the Fool and for Kent. The Fool ends with a poem about wrong and right.

Act three, Scene 3

Gloucester confides in Edmund that there is a rebellion against Albany and Cornwall being planned. He tells Edmund to talk to the Duke

Introduction to the Play

and say that he has gone to bed so that his negative feelings toward Cornwall will not be evident. He leaves, and Edmund immediately admits that he will tell everything his father said to the Duke, even though it betrays his father.

Act three, Scene 4

Kent leads Lear and the Fool to the hovel. Lear thinks about all he has done for Goneril and Regan, and it almost makes him go mad. As Lear surveys the storm, he begins to realize that he has not paid attention to those less fortunate than he.

Inside the hovel, they meet up with Edgar, who is acting as a deranged beggar, Tom O' Bedlam. Tom speaks in a crazy way about his condition. Lear sees Edgar as "unaccommodated man." Realizing that he, too, is not more than a "poor, bare, forked animal," Lear begins to rip off his clothes.

Gloucester finds everyone at the hovel. Even though it will get him into trouble, he has come to lead Lear back to his castle. Edgar recognizes his father and continues to act as if he has lost his mind. Gloucester, thinking that Edgar is homeless, tells Edgar to stay in the hovel, but King Lear insists that Edgar stay with him, calling him a philosopher.

Act three, Scene 5

Edmund shows the Duke of Cornwall the letter from Gloucester that speaks of treason against Cornwall. Edmund pretends that he is sad that he has to be the one to expose his father. The Duke of Cornwall states that he will replace Edmund as the Duke of Gloucester.

Act three, Scene 6

In a room on Gloucester's estate, King Lear, Kent, the Fool, and Edgar wait out the storm. King Lear appears to be in a psychotic state. Kent asks him to rest, but Lear insists on a trial. He puts his two oldest daughters on trial, and uses a joint stool to represent Goneril. The Fool, Edgar, and Kent stand as judges. Edgar feels so sorry for King Lear that he says in an aside that it is difficult for him to keep from crying. After a wild and passionate trial, Lear sleeps.

Gloucester enters and asks Kent to take Lear to Dover because there is a plot to kill the King. Edgar remains behind and gives a brief soliloquy admitting that his problems seem small compared to the suffering of King Lear.

Act three, Scene 7

Regan and Cornwall decide to punish Gloucester for aiding King Lear and for siding with France against their rule. They tie Gloucester to a chair in order to put out his eyes. Cornwall's servant tries to save him and wounds Cornwall. Regan grabs a sword and kills the servant. During the horrible, cruel blinding, Gloucester comes to realize that Edmund betrayed him and that Edgar was indeed a true and loyal son. Cornwall and Regan leave, and two remaining servants dress Gloucester's eyes and plan to get Tom O' Bedlam to lead Gloucester to wherever he wants to go, not realizing that Tom is Edgar in disguise.

Introduction to the Play

Act four, Scene 1

An old man leads Gloucester to Edgar. Edgar is overwhelmed at his father's condition. Gloucester is in a state of extreme despair, saying, "As flies to wanton boys are we to the gods; they kill us for their sport." Gloucester also expresses a wish to be reunited with Edgar, saying, "Might I but live to see thee in my touch, I'd say I had eyes again." Gloucester asks Edgar to lead him to the cliffs of Dover so that he can pitch himself off the cliff and end his misery. Edgar agrees, saying, "Poor Tom shall lead thee."

Act four, Scene 2

Oswald reports to Goneril and Edmund that the Duke of Albany is not happy with what is happening in the kingdom. Goneril expresses to Edmund that she wishes Edmund were her husband, carrying both rank and position. Edmund and Goneril kiss, and Edmund leaves for the Duke of Cornwall's estate. The Duke of Albany enters and expresses his displeasure at the vile treatment of King Lear. Goneril calls Albany "milk-livered" and states that he is wasting his pity on those villains while France is threatening their own kingdom. Albany replies that Goneril has become a monster, and if it were an appropriate behavior for a man, he would kill her as he would kill a fiend. Goneril demeans Albany for calling himself a man. They are interrupted by a messenger who announces that the Duke of Cornwall has died from the injuries he received from his servant during the blinding of Gloucester. Albany is shocked at the torture of Gloucester and aligns himself with Gloucester against his own wife, Goneril. Meanwhile, Goneril is worried that, with Cornwall dead, her sister may make a play for Edmund.

Act four, Scene 3

Kent speaks with the Gentleman about why the King of France has turned away from England and returned to France. He has left the Marshal of France to carry on the attack against the British kingdom. Kent asks how Cordelia received the news of her father's situation. The Gentleman reports that Cordelia cried and uttered words of shame against her sisters. Kent then says that Lear refuses to meet with Cordelia because he is too ashamed of how he disinherited her and raised up her two older, evil sisters.

Act four, Scene 4

In the French camp near Dover, Cordelia hopes for some herbs to sooth her father's madness. The doctor replies that what Lear needs most is true rest, which Lear is unable to do. A messenger announces that the British powers are marching toward them. Cordelia does not seek to be victorious for her own gain, but in order to show her love to her father.

Act four, Scene 5

Regan tells Oswald, Goneril's servant, that it was a mistake to let Gloucester live because he turns people's hearts against their cause. Edmund, however, is hoping to find and kill Gloucester. Regan expresses her displeasure at Goneril for wanting to marry Edmund, since she is a widow and is legally free to marry.

Introduction to the Play

Act four, Scene 6

Edgar leads the blind Gloucester to a small hill, telling Gloucester that he is on the edge of the steep cliffs of Dover. Gloucester kneels, prays to the gods, and blesses Edgar. He pitches himself forward, thinking he is falling off the cliff. Edgar changes his voice to impersonate a fisherman. He tells his father that a divine monster was with Gloucester at the top of the cliff, and that he floated to the ground. Gloucester, believing his life is a miracle, vows not to commit suicide. Lear arrives, and in crazy, disjointed language, laments his condition. He speaks with disgust about his daughters and all women as sexually debased. During his tirade about justice and self-awareness, he recognizes Gloucester. In despair at Gloucester's eyes, Lear speaks the memorable lines, "When we are born, we cry that we are come/To this great stage of fools."

Some men enter and attempt to bring Lear to Cordelia. Lear thinks they are trying to arrest him, and he runs away. Oswald comes upon Gloucester and Edgar and tries to slay Gloucester. Using a disguised voice, Edgar defends his father and kills Oswald. As he dies, Oswald asks Edgar to give his letters to Edmund. Edgar reads the letter from Goneril to Edmund. In it, she asks him to kill Albany and make the situation look like an accident of war, and she calls herself the wife of Edmund. Edgar states that he will tell Albany of his wife's evil plot against him at the right time. Gloucester envies King Lear because in his madness he is unaware of the evil around him.

Act four, Scene 7

Cordelia thanks Kent for assisting her father and asks him to get out of his disguise. She asks the doctors how her father is doing, and they say that he is sleeping. They have given him fresh clothes. The doctors bring in the sleeping Lear, and Cordelia kisses him to wake him up. As Lear is waking up, she wonders at the cruelty of her sisters.

As Lear wakes up, he thinks at first that Cordelia is an angel and he is a soul in hell. Lear tries to kneel before her. Sane, King Lear recognizes Cordelia and asks her forgiveness. Reunited, they go for a walk.

Act five, Scene 1

Regan asks Edmund if he has committed adultery with Goneril, and Edmund says he has only honorable love for Regan's sister. The Duke of Albany and Goneril enter, and Regan asks Goneril to accompany her so that Goneril will not have an opportunity to be alone with Edmund. Goneril understands Regan's motives and accompanies her sister. Edgar enters in disguise and asks Albany to read the letter that shows his wife's treachery. Edgar says he must leave, but he will reappear if Albany sounds the herald. Everyone leaves except Edmund. He wonders which sister he will have once he has killed Albany. He states that he will offer no mercy to King Lear and Cordelia if they are captured.

Introduction to the Play

Act five, Scene 2

Edgar tells his father that Lear and Cordelia have been captured. Gloucester asks to sit and rot, but Edgar tells him that men must endure their lives, even though they are grim.

Act five, Scene 3

Edmund leads in the prisoners King Lear and Cordelia. Cordelia says to Lear that she is not sad for herself but for Lear's situation. Lear says that he is happy about prison since he can be with Cordelia. Edmund gives an officer a note that orders the death of Cordelia.

Albany, Goneril, Regan, and some soldiers enter. Goneril and Regan argue over Regan's wish to marry Edmund. Albany stops the fight by saying that Edmund is arrested for treason. Albany says that if no one comes to challenge Edmund, he will duel with Edmund himself. Regan becomes increasingly sick, and Albany orders his men to bring her to his tent. Goneril, in an aside, implies that she has poisoned her sister.

At the sound of the herald, Edgar arrives to fight Edmund, calling him a traitor to his brother, to his father, and to everyone. Edgar stabs Edmund, but Albany cries out to Edgar not to kill Edmund so that he may stand trial for treason. Albany confronts Goneril with her letter to Edmund, and she leaves.

Edgar reveals himself to Edmund and Albany. He tells them how he disguised himself as Tom O' Bedlam. He explains that he just revealed himself to Gloucester, who died from being overwhelmed by Edgar's loyalty and love.

A gentleman comes in to announce that Goneril has killed herself and that Regan is also dead from Goneril's poison. Their bodies are brought in, and Edmund expresses sadness that he has lost their love. He then tries to reverse his letter ordering the death of Cordelia, to do one good thing before he dies from his wound.

Edmund, however, is too late. Lear enters carrying the body of Cordelia. He attempts to find out if she is still alive, but he realizes she is dead. In his rage, Lear killed the slave who was hanging Cordelia. He speaks with Kent, who tells Lear that Goneril and Regan are also dead. A messenger enters and announces that Edmund is dead.

Lear, thinking that Cordelia's lips are moving and that she is alive, becomes overwhelmed and dies. Kent tells everyone to let Lear go because he has suffered enough. Albany asks Kent and Edgar to help him rule the kingdom, but Kent implies that he will kill himself. Edgar speaks the final words of sadness and suffering: "We that are young/Shall never see so much nor live so long."

Annotated Character List for *King Lear*

King Lear: A ruler of the pre-Christian British kingdom. He wishes to give up the cares and responsibilities of ruling while enjoying a comfortable retirement in the care of his daughters. His abdication of the throne and his division of the kingdom is his undoing.

Goneril: The eldest daughter of King Lear. She is married to the Scottish Duke of Albany. She is quick to use flowery language of love to her father when she thinks it will gain her

Introduction to the Play

a greater share of the kingdom. She quickly turns against her father, however, once she has money and power. Becoming ever more jealous and evil, she eventually poisons her own sister.

Regan: She is similar to her elder sister in nature. She is married to the Duke of Cornwall. Because it serves her purposes, she never hesitates as she locks her father out on a stormy knight or tortures and blinds the Earl of Gloucester.

Cordelia: The youngest daughter of King Lear. Although she does not speak fancy words of love to her father, she is a very loyal and loving daughter. She marries the King of France and comes to her father's rescue. Her love will pay the greatest price.

The Duke of Albany: The husband of Goneril. When he realizes the evil being done by his wife and her sister, he rejects their wickedness.

The Duke of Cornwall: The husband of Regan. He is her partner in all things wicked and evil. He initiates the barring of the door against King Lear and the torture of Gloucester. He is stabbed by one of his own servants during the torture of Gloucester and dies soon after from that wound.

The King of France: He is happy to marry Cordelia even after she loses her inheritance. He helps to launch the rescue of King Lear, but he is not present at the final battle.

The Duke of Burgundy: When offered the hand of Cordelia in marriage after she is penniless, he turns her down.

The Earl of Kent: A loyal supporter of King Lear. Even though he was banished for telling the truth, he disguises himself as a servant in order to continue to be of service to the King.

The Earl of Gloucester: An earl in the court of King Lear. He has two sons, one from his wife and the other from his mistress. Because his illegitimate son fools him, he rejects his true son. His part in the revolt against Lear's two daughters causes him extreme suffering and despair.

Edmund: Gloucester's illegitimate son. He is full of evil and jealously, and he is willing to stop at nothing to have all the rights and privileges of a legitimate son. At the very end of his life, he tries to redeem his behavior, but it is too late.

Edgar: The legitimate son and heir of the Earl of Gloucester. He is falsely accused by Edmund of planning his father's murder. To avoid being harmed by his father, he disguises himself as a crazy, homeless beggar, Tom O'Bedlam.

Oswald: The steward of Goneril; he often participates in her evil plots.

A Knight: One of King Lear's retinue

The Fool: A court jester who uses riddle and rhyme to show Lear that he is being foolish

Curan: A steward in Gloucester's household

Gentleman: Talks with Kent about the condition of King Lear in Act three

Old Man: A longtime tenant of Gloucester's manor; he leads Gloucester to the disguised Edgar after Gloucester has been blinded.

Introduction to the Play

Messengers: They bring news of the progress of the battle.

Doctor: Employed by Cordelia to help in the restoration and healing of King Lear

Two Captains: They lead the battles of France and England.

Herald: He sounds a trumpet so that Edgar will come forward and challenge Edmund.

Other Minor Characters: knights, attendants, servants, officers, soldiers, and trumpeters

Shakespeare and Stage Directions

The plays of Shakespeare are so well written that they seem to leap off the page and come to life. However, the plays themselves have very few stage directions. Perhaps this is because Shakespeare's plays were performed in large amphitheaters that were very simple.

This was a time before electric lights, so the plays needed to take place during the day to utilize the natural light. The average time for a performance was between noon and two in the afternoon. Theater historians report that there were typically no intermissions; plays ran from beginning to end without a break and took about two hours.

The set might be painted canvas to illustrate whether the play was occurring in a forest or a town, for example. Sometimes the background was accompanied by a sign that indicated the place as well. Props were few and large: a table, a chariot, gallows, a bed, or a throne.

However, the audience in Shakespeare's plays expected a spectacle for the price of admission. Therefore, there were many devices to produce a gasp from the audience. For example, a device in the loft of the theater could raise and lower actors so that they could play gods, ghosts, or other unusual characters. Additionally, a trapdoor in the stage offered a chance for a quick appearance or disappearance. The actors could suggest a beheading or hanging with various illusions on the stage. Sound effects suggesting thunder, horses, or war were common. Music was important, and drums and horns were often played.

Most important to the sense of spectacle were the costumes worn by the actors. These were elaborate, colorful, and very expensive. Therefore, they often purchased these outfits from servants who had inherited the clothes from their masters, or from hangmen, who received the clothes of their victims as payment for their services.

Though Shakespeare's stage directions are sparse, definition of a few key terms will be helpful for the reader. The following is a brief glossary of stage directions commonly found in Shakespeare's plays.

Selected Glossary of Stage Directions in Shakespeare's Plays

Above: an indication that the actor speaking from above is on a higher balcony or other scaffold that is higher than the other actors

Alarum: a stage signal, which calls the soldiers to battle; usually trumpets, drums, and shouts

Aside: words spoken by the actor so the audience overhears but the other actors on the stage do not. An aside may also be spoken to one

Introduction to the Play

other actor so that the others on stage do not overhear.

Calls within: a voice offstage that calls to a character on the stage

Curtains: Curtains were fabrics draped around a bed that could be opened or closed for privacy.

Draw: Actors pull their swords from their sheathes.

Enter: a direction for a character to enter the stage. This can be from the audience's right (stage right) or the audience's left (stage left).

Enter Chorus: a direction for an actor to come to the center of the stage and offer some introductory comments, usually in blank verse or rhyming couplets. In *Romeo and Juliet*, the Chorus delivers a sonnet, a form of poetry associated with love.

Exeunt: All characters leave the stage, or those characters named leave the stage.

Exit: One character leaves the stage.

Flourish: A group of trumpets or other horn instruments play a brief melody.

Have at: Characters begin to fight, usually with swords.

Pageant: a show or spectacle of actors in unusual costumes, usually without words

Prologue: an introduction spoken by the Chorus that gives an overview to the audience and invites them into the play or scene

Retires: A character slips away.

Sennet: a series of notes sounded on brass instruments to announce the approach or departure of a procession

Singing: a signal for the actor to sing the following lines as a tune

Within: voices or sounds occurring offstage but heard by the audience

Introduction to Shakespeare

A Brief Biography of William Shakespeare

William Shakespeare was born in April 1564 to John and Mary Shakespeare in Stratford-upon-Avon, England. His birthday is celebrated on April 23. This is memorable because April 23 is also the day Shakespeare died in 1616.

Shakespeare was the eldest of nine children in his family, six of whom survived to adulthood.

William Shakespeare's father worked with leather and became a successful merchant early in his career. He held some relatively important government offices. However, when William was in his early teens, his father's financial position began to slide due to growing debt. After many years, John Shakespeare's fortunes and respect were restored, but records indicate that the years of debt and lawsuits were very stressful.

Historians assume that young Will went to school and took a rigorous course of study including Latin, history, and biblical study. In 1582, at the age of eighteen, he married Anne Hathaway, who was three months pregnant. Studies of Elizabethan family life indicate that Anne's situation was not unusual since it was accepted that the engagement period was as legally binding as the marriage. The couple had a daughter, Susanna, followed by twins, Hamnet and Judith. Not much is known about Shakespeare during the next seven years, but his name is listed as an actor in London by 1592. This was a difficult time for the theater because measures to prevent the spread of the plague regularly closed the theaters.

Between 1594 and 1595, Shakespeare joined the Chamberlain's Men as a playwright and actor. The acting company featured actor Richard Burbage, and they were a favorite of Queen Elizabeth I. During this time, Shakespeare was writing such plays as *Romeo and Juliet* and *A Midsummer Night's Dream*. Even though Shakespeare was enjoying great success by the time he was 32, it was dampened by the death of his son, Hamnet, in 1596. Soon after, Shakespeare refocused on his home in Stratford where he bought an estate called New Place, with gardens, orchards, and barns in addition to the main home. He still maintained a home in London near the theater.

In 1599, Shakespeare wrote *Henry V*, *Julius Caesar*, and *As You Like It*. The Globe Playhouse was up and running, with Shakespeare a 10 percent owner. This means that he was able to earn 10 percent of any show's profits. This business position helped him solidify his wealth.

In 1603, Shakespeare's reputation earned his acting troop the sponsorship of James I, who requested one play performance per month. Their name changed to the King's Men. By this time, Shakespeare had written and performed in almost all of his comedies and histories. He was proclaimed the finest playwright in London.

Introduction to Shakespeare

But Shakespeare still had what is considered his finest writing to do. He began his writing of tragedies beginning with *Hamlet* in 1600. In the following five years, Shakespeare wrote *Macbeth*, *Othello*, and *King Lear*. Why Shakespeare turned to these darker, more serious themes is widely debated by scholars. But all agree that these plays established Shakespeare's premier place in English literature.

Toward the end of 1609 through 1610, Shakespeare began to write his problem romances. These works, *The Winter's Tale*, *Cymbeline*, and *The Tempest*, are rich with mature themes of forgiveness, grace, and redemption.

After 1611, at the age of 47, Shakespeare moved back to Stratford exclusively, settling into life at New Place and enjoying a renewed relationship with his daughters, especially Susanna. He prepared a will, which has become famous for the request to leave his wife their "second best bed." Many have debated whether this is a sentimental or cynical bequest. In the same year that his daughter Judith married, 1616, Shakespeare died at the age of 52. However, it was not until 1623 that all his plays were collected into one manuscript, now referred to as the *First Folio*. The fellow King's Men players who compiled the manuscript, Heming and Condell, entitled it *Mr. William Shakespeare's Comedies, Histories, and Tragedies*.

Shakespeare's England

The age of Shakespeare was a glorious time for England. William Shakespeare's life in England was defined by the reign of Queen Elizabeth I (1558–1603). During her leadership, England became an important naval and economic force in Europe and beyond.

England's rise to power came when its navy defeated the Spanish Armada in 1588, when Shakespeare was about 24 years old. Queen Elizabeth was skillful in navigating through the conflicts of religion. She maintained religious independence from Rome as the Church of England became firmly rooted during her reign. Additionally, she financed the establishment of colonies in America to grow the British Empire and expand its economic opportunities. At the end of her reign, England was the leader in trade, naval power, and culture.

Because of its role as the main economic, political, and cultural center of England, London became the hub of England's prosperity and fame. If anyone wanted to become famous as a poet or dramatic writer during Shakespeare's time, he would need to be in London. In fact, London was full of great writers besides Shakespeare, such as Marlowe, Sidney, and Jonson. Yet, even as London was full of parties, trade, and amusement, it was also full of poverty, crime, and disease. Crime was a large problem, and the main jail in London was called the Clink. Disease and poor sanitation were common. In fact, twice in Shakespeare's lifetime, London endured an outbreak of the plague, which killed thousands upon thousands of people.

Before Queen Elizabeth took the throne, London was a modestly sized city of about 60,000 people. By the time James I took the throne at her death, more than 200,000 people

Introduction to Shakespeare

lived in London and its suburbs. People were attracted to London because it gave many opportunities for work and financial improvement. It was also a vibrant social scene for the upper class. In fact, one honor of being a noble was the opportunity to house Queen Elizabeth and her entire party if she was in your neighborhood. If she was a guest, it was expected that her noble hosts would cover all the expenses of housing her group. She made many "progresses" through England and London, establishing her relationships with the nobility. However, several nobles asked to be released from this honor because the expense of supporting her visit had often caused them bankruptcy.

Perhaps it was better to be a flourishing member of the English merchant middle class. Their numbers and influence were rising in England at the time of Shakespeare. This was a new and an exciting development in Western European history. One major factor in the rise of the middle class was the need for wool for clothing. The expansion of the wool trade led to the formation of entire cities throughout England, and sparked progress in many other areas of commerce and trade.

With the rise of the middle class came a concern for more comfortable housing. Rather than serving simply as shelter or defense against attack, housing developed architecturally and functionally. One major improvement was the use of windows to let in light. Also, houses were built with lofts and special places for eating and sleeping, rather than having one multifunctional room. However, doors between rooms were still very rare, so that privacy in Shakespeare's time did not really exist.

Meals in Shakespeare's England were an important part of the day. Breakfast was served before dawn and was usually bread and a beverage. Therefore, everyone was really hungry for the midday meal, which could last up to three hours. If meat was available in the home, it was usually served at this time. A smaller supper was eaten at 6:00 or 7:00 P.M., with the more wealthy people able to eat earlier and the working class eating later. Cooking was dangerous and difficult since all meals were cooked over an open fire. Even bread was not baked in an oven but was cooked in special pans placed over the fire. A pot was almost always cooking on the fire, and the cook would put in whatever was available for supper. This is most likely where the term "potluck" came from.

Furniture was usually made of carved wood, as woodcarving was a developing craft in Shakespeare's day. One important part of an Elizabethan home was the table, or "board." One side was finished to a nice sheen, while the other side was rough. Meals were served on the rough side of the board, and then it was flipped for a more elegant look in the room. The table is where we get the terms "room and board" and having "the tables turned." Another important part of a middle or an upper-class home was the bed. Rather than being made of prickly straw, mattresses were now stuffed with softer feathers. Surrounded by artistically carved four posts, these beds were considered so valuable that they were often a specifically named item in a will.

Introduction to Shakespeare

Clothing in Shakespeare's time was very expensive. Of course, servants and other lower-class people wore simple garb, often a basic blue. But if a person wanted to display his wealth, his clothing was elaborate and colorful, sewn with rich velvet, lace, and gold braid. An average worker might earn seven or eight English pounds in a year, and a very nice outfit for a nobleman might cost as much as 50 or 60 pounds. In other words, if seven or eight healthy workers pooled their money for the entire year, spending nothing else, they could buy only one respectable nobleman's outfit.

Entertainment was an important part of life in Shakespeare's England. Popular sports were bear-baiting, cockfighting, and an early form of bowling. Bear-baiting, in which a dog was set loose to fight with up to three chained bears in the center of an amphitheater, and cockfighting, in which roosters pecked each other to death, were popular then but would be absolutely unacceptable entertainment today. Bowling, however, has maintained its popularity in our current culture.

In London, a main source of entertainment was the theater. Some theaters were very large and could hold more than two thousand people. Even poor people could attend the theater since entrance cost only one penny (equivalent to 60 cents today), and they could stand around the stage. For a bit more money, a person could sit in an actual seat during the performance. However, some thought that going to the theater could be dangerous to your body or your soul. The theaters were closed twice during the plagues to reduce the spread of the disease. The Puritans disapproved of the theater as an unwholesome leisure time activity. And the Puritans also disliked the theater because the theaters were located in an area of London surrounded by brothels and bars. Nevertheless, the theater became respectable enough by 1603 to be supported by James I—and he was the monarch who directed the King James Version of the Bible to be translated.

# ACTIVITY 1
Honesty Versus Flattery

Act one, Scene 1

Background In this scene, King Lear announces his plan to separate his kingdom into three parts. He asks his daughters to express to him how much they love him so that he may determine who deserves the most land in his kingdom. His two elder daughters, Regan and Goneril, lavish him with melodramatic sentiments of their love, and he gives them the second and third largest shares of land, saving the largest part for his youngest (and favorite) daughter. Cordelia disappoints the king with her straightforward sentiment; although the reader understands that she is the only one who truly loves her father with the utmost devotion, she is sincere and humble and not given to flattery. Her father is outraged, gives Cordelia's portion of his kingdom to Regan and Goneril, and disinherits Cordelia, banishing her from the kingdom.

Directions In modern-day speech, write three brief speeches that parallel what the three daughters say to their father. Immediately after each speech, write whatever "secret" thoughts each young woman may have been thinking either before, during, or after her speech. Use another sheet of paper, if necessary.

Goneril's speech:

Goneril's secret thoughts:

Regan's speech:

Regan's secret thoughts:

Cordelia's speech:

Cordelia's secret thoughts:

© 2004 Walch Publishing   1   *Shakespeare Made Easy: King Lear*

ACTIVITY 2

Deception Everywhere

Act one

Background There is much deception in this act, and no one seems to do anything for pure motives except Cordelia.

Directions Describe the deception that each character is planning in this act. Though we cannot confirm the King of France's deception, carefully consider what the King of France could gain by marrying Cordelia, even if she is initially cast off by her temperamental father. For each character, list the approximate lines in which you discovered the deception.

King of France (speculate):

Edmund:

Goneril and Regan:

Kent:

ACTIVITY 3
Goneril and Regan Deal with Dad

Act one, Scenes 3–5

Background After lavishing him with compliments to get a better inheritance, Goneril and Regan are now forced to live with their father and his one hundred knights. There is much friction between Goneril and her father, and this will carry over to Regan. Goneril claims that the knights are badly behaved, but Lear disputes this. Who is to blame here? Is Goneril wrong to feel frustrated with her father's large entourage? You decide.

Directions Reread Scenes 3–5 and examine Lear's attitude toward Goneril and her servants and Goneril's attitude toward Lear and his knights. Then

1. Decide who is to blame for the conflict, and try to cite at least three quotations per character.

2. Write one of the following letters from your chosen character's perspective:

    a. a letter from Goneril to Regan telling Regan what has happened with Lear and what she has done about it

    b. a letter from Lear to Regan complaining about his treatment at Goneril's castle

    c. a letter from Regan to Lear expressing her frustration

Use another sheet of paper for your letter.

Part 1: Who is to blame/Character Quotations:

Part 2: Letter from _____ to _____

© 2004 Walch Publishing   *Shakespeare Made Easy: King Lear*

ACTIVITY 4
The Jester Who Told the Truth

Act one, Scene 4

Background In King Lear's day, court jesters were comedian-entertainers, or simply dim-witted persons kept as objects for entertainment. Lear's jester (or Fool) is privileged in that he is allowed to speak the truth to the King, which he often does comically, sarcastically, and with use of irony.

Directions The Fool frequently insults King Lear in this scene, yet the King does not punish him for it. Write the following insults/insinuations by the Fool about or to Lear in your own words. Use another sheet of paper, if necessary.

1. "Why, this fellow has banished two on's daughters, and did the third a blessing against his will: if thou follow him thou must needs wear my coxcomb."

2. "Leave thy drink and thy whore/And keep in-a-door,/And thou shalt have more/Than two tens to a score."

3. "That lord that counselled thee/To give away thy land,/Come place him here by me;/Do thou for him stand:/The sweet and bitter fool/Will presently appear;/The one in motley here,/The other found out there."

4. "When thou clovest thy crown i' th' middle, and gavest away both parts, thou borest thine ass on thy back o'er the dirt: thou hadst little wit in thy bald crown when thou gavest thy golden one away."

ACTIVITY 5
Review

Directions   Answer the following questions. Write the letter of the correct answer in the space provided. For 8, write true (T) or false (F) in the space provided.

___ 1. King Lear is king of what country?
   a. Italy
   b. France
   c. Britain
   d. Denmark

___ 2. Who is Gloucester's illegitimate child?
   a. Edgar
   b. Edmund
   c. Kent
   d. Cornwall

___ 3. Why does King Lear disown Cordelia?
   a. He has run out of money.
   b. She deceived him earlier.
   c. Her answer about how much she loves him displeases him.
   d. She conspired behind his back for a greater inheritance.

___ 4. Who tries to defend Cordelia, only to get in trouble himself?
   a. Oswald
   b. Kent
   c. Gloucester
   d. Regan

___ 5. Who says that he wants to marry Cordelia, despite the fact that she is disinherited?
   a. Duke of Burgandy
   b. King of France
   c. Kent
   d. Edmund

___ 6. Does Cordelia love her father less than her sisters do?
   a. Yes
   b. No

___ 7. How does King Lear punish Kent?
   a. execution
   b. banishment
   c. revoking his title
   d. taking his land

___ 8. True or false: Regan and Goneril are plotting to take Lear's power (throne) from him.

___ 9. How does Edmund scheme against his brother?
   a. He shows his father a letter that he forged in Edgar's handwriting.
   b. He has hired someone to kill him.
   c. He is planning to kill him.
   d. none of the above

___ 10. How many knights does Lear insist on keeping when he divides his kingdom?
   a. ten
   b. fifty
   c. one hundred
   d. two hundred

ACTIVITY 6
Shakespearean Insults

Act two, Scene 2

Background In this scene, Kent picks a fight with Oswald and insults him very rudely and profusely. In Shakespeare's day, insulting someone was a sort of art form, and Kent's insults to Oswald show great inventiveness.

Directions Using Shakespearean language as best you can, and drawing from Kent's bounty of insults or any other Shakespearean play with which you might be familiar, imagine that you are an enraged (rather than frightened) Oswald defending yourself. Compose a brief speech during which you answer and surpass all of Kent's insults. Provide a paraphrase or an explanation of your speech in modern English as well. Use another sheet of paper, if necessary.

ACTIVITY 7
Poor Edgar

Act two, Scene 3

Background Edgar has been badly wronged by his half-brother, Edmund, but he may not realize it yet. Review what has happened in Act one, Scene 2 and Act two, Scenes 1 and 3.

Directions Imagine that you are Edgar and compose a letter to your father (Gloucester), explaining that you are innocent of the charges heaped upon you. Plead for your life and your reinstatement, and describe what you think has happened to cause this misunderstanding. Suggested length: ¾ of a page to 1 page. Use another sheet of paper, if necessary.

ACTIVITY 8
The King Breaks Down

Act two, Scene 4

Background When both Regan and Goneril turn against their father and demand that he keep only twenty-five men because he doesn't really need even one, Lear's response is very telling.

Directions Answer the following questions based on King Lear's speech to his daughters when they have told him that he really does not need even one follower.

1. "O, reason not the need; our basest beggars/Are in the poorest thing superfluous:/Allow not nature more than nature needs,/Man's life's as cheap as beast's."

    Question: What is Lear saying about what makes a man happy and separates him from animals?

2. "Thou art a lady;/If only to go warm were gorgeous,/Why, nature needs not what thou gorgeous wear'st,/Which scarcely keeps thee warm."

    Question: How does Lear compare his daughters' material needs to his in order to make his point about "needing" followers?

3. Do you think Regan and Goneril are acting selfishly, or is this whole conflict King Lear's fault? Why?

4. Why is King Lear so hurt by his daughters' not allowing him his entourage?

5. Do you think that Regan and Goneril are right in not stopping their father from going out in the storm? Why or why not?

ACTIVITY 9
Courtly Reporter

Acts one and two

Background Much of what happens in Acts one and two sets up the themes of the entire play. Some events take place in public, while others are private occurrences.

Directions Imagine that you write a gazette that focuses on the daily occurrences in Britain's royal court. Decide which events from each of the acts are important enough to warrant a write-up in your paper. Then write an article incorporating those events, making sure to mention the people involved. Suggested length: $\frac{1}{2}$ of a page to 1 page. Use another sheet of paper, if necessary.

ACTIVITY 10
Review

Directions Test your understanding of the characters thus far by matching each character with the correct description of him or her. Write the letter of the correct character in the space provided.

    a. Gloucester   d. Oswald   g. King Lear   j. King of France
    b. Cordelia   e. Kent   h. Goneril
    c. Edgar   f. Edmund   i. Cornwall

_____ 1. plots against his half-brother

_____ 2. was disowned by her father

_____ 3. Edgar's father

_____ 4. disguises himself in order to stay in the King's service

_____ 5. Lear's eldest daughter

_____ 6. gets abused physically and verbally by Kent

_____ 7. pretends he is a beggar to protect his life

_____ 8. wants to retain his one hundred knights

_____ 9. Regan's husband

_____ 10. marries penniless Cordelia

ACTIVITY 11
Civil War in Britain?

Act three, Scene 1

Background We have read rumors of anger between Cornwall and Albany, but now Kent confirms it to the Gentleman.

Directions Answer the following questions about Kent's discussion with the Gentleman in order to better understand whether or not Cornwall and Albany will go to war and whether or not France will be involved in the fray.

1. Find the specific line in which Kent tells the Gentleman that there is, indeed, a feud between Albany and Cornwall. Write the quotation in the space provided.

2. What are the three possible subjects about which the servants of Cornwall and Albany are spying and reporting to the King of France?

   a.

   b.

   c.

3. What is France prepared to do?

4. Why does Kent give his ring to the Gentleman?

5. Whom do they go looking for at the end of their conversation?

© 2004 Walch Publishing

Shakespeare Made Easy: King Lear

ACTIVITY 12
Predictions

Act three

Background Good readers not only periodically review what they have read, they also predict what is to come. Act three is a critical point in the play for many characters, and many of them are facing perilous situations.

Directions Predict what will happen to each of the following characters based on your knowledge of what has happened so far and your intuition as to what will occur next.

1. King Lear has been shut out in a terrible storm by his two daughters, he has no followers except the Fool, and he seems to be losing his grip on reality. What will happen to King Lear?

2. Edgar is an outlaw, currently pretending to be a mad beggar, seeking to right his reputation from the lies his brother convinced everyone of. What will happen to him?

3. Kent is disguised as a servant of King Lear, but he has partially revealed himself to a Gentleman who is to carry a message to Cordelia. He has alienated himself from Regan and Cornwall by being rude to Oswald, and now he is trying to keep King Lear safe. What will happen to him?

4. Gloucester has been betrayed by Edmund, blinded and pushed out into the cold, and thought to be a spy for France. What will happen to him?

© 2004 Walch Publishing · *Shakespeare Made Easy: King Lear*

ACTIVITY 13

Words of Wisdom from a "Madman" Act three, Scene 6

Background Amid all the turmoil, Edgar takes a moment to pause and say some wise words about suffering.

Directions First, write Edgar's speech in your own words, and then speculate about why, before he was an outcast, he would not have understood the depth and significance of what King Lear is experiencing. Use another sheet of paper, if necessary.

When we our betters see bearing our woes,
We scarcely think our miseries our foes.
Who alone suffers, suffers most i' th' mind,
Leaving free things and happy shows behind;
But then the mind much sufferance do o'erskip,
When grief hath mates, and bearing fellowship.
How light and portable my pain seems now,
When that which makes me bend makes the
    King bow;

He childed as I fathered! Tom, away!
Mark the high noises, and thyself bewray
When false opinion, whose wrong thoughts
    defile thee,
In thy just proof repeals and reconciles three.
What will hap more to-night, safe 'scape the
    King!
Lurk, lurk.

Your paraphrase:

Why do you think Edgar truly understands and has empathy for King Lear now (as opposed to before he was betrayed and labeled an outlaw)?

© 2004 Walch Publishing   13   *Shakespeare Made Easy: King Lear*

ACTIVITY 14
Event Recall

Act three

Background Much occurs in Act three, and many of the main characters of the play meet up in unusual circumstances.

Directions Read the following five passages/lines, which serve as clues to seven different events occurring in this act. Then, on another sheet of paper, write one sentence per event that identifies and briefly explains the importance of each event.

Event 1 clue: "[The King is] Contending with the fretful elements; . . . Strives in his little world of man to out-scorn/The to-and-fro-conflicting wind and rain./This night, wherein the cub-drawn bear would couch,/the lion and the belly-pinched wolf/Keep their fur dry, unbonneted he runs,/And bids what will take all." (spoken by the Gentleman in Scene 1)

Event 2 clue: "These injuries the King now bears will be revenged home; there is part of a power already footed; we must incline to the King." (spoken by Gloucester in Scene 3)

(continued)

ACTIVITY 14

Event Recall (continued)

Event 3 clue: "This courtesy, forbid thee, shall the Duke/Instantly know, and of that letter too:/This seems a fair deserving, and must draw me/That which my father loses; no less than all:/The younger rises when the old doth fall." (spoken by Edmund in Scene 3)

Event 4 clue: "Pluck out his eyes." (spoken by Goneril in Scene 7)

Event 5 clue: "I have received a hurt . . . Regan, I bleed apace:/Untimely comes this hurt. Give me your arm." (spoken by Cornwall in Scene 7)

ACTIVITY 15
Review

Directions Read each statement and decide if it is true or false. Then write true (T) or false (F) in the space provided.

_____ 1. Kent gives the Gentleman a ring to give to Cordelia.

_____ 2. King Lear is going mad (insane).

_____ 3. The Fool abandoned King Lear when faced with being out in the storm.

_____ 4. Edmund betrays his father to Cornwall.

_____ 5. Gloucester cares for the King.

_____ 6. Gloucester is killed for betraying Cornwall, Regan, and Goneril.

_____ 7. Cornwall is wounded by Gloucester.

_____ 8. Gloucester is blinded.

_____ 9. The servants are loyal to Cornwall and Regan.

_____ 10. Gloucester recognizes his banished son, Edgar.

ACTIVITY 16
Father and Son Reunion

Act four, Scene 1

Background   Shakespeare paints a touching scene here, with the blinded and ousted Gloucester unknowingly being reunited with his wronged son, Edgar, who is pretending to be a mad beggar. He even wishes aloud (in Edgar's presence) that he could just touch his son once again. Edgar is too overcome to respond to his father, and he keeps up his disguise as a way to hide his emotions.

Directions   Add a scene in which Edgar tells his father who he is. Write it in play format (Gloucester speaks, Edgar speaks, and so forth). Suggested length: 1 page. Use another sheet of paper, if necessary.

ACTIVITY 17

Answered Letter

Act four, Scene 2

Background Seeing her own husband as weak and incapable, the scheming and unfaithful Goneril has made an alliance with Edmund, who has wronged both his father and half-brother. Now, she finds out through a messenger that her sister's husband (Cornwall) has died. War is imminent, and Goneril wants the kingdom for herself, so she needs to defeat France's army. She is concerned that her hopes for the kingdom could be ruined now that Regan is a widow and might try to claim Edmund for herself. She needs to carefully craft a response to the letter brought by the messenger from Regan.

Directions Write Goneril's letter of response to her sister Regan. Suggested length: ½ of a page to ¾ of a page. Use another sheet of paper, if necessary. Keep in mind the following:

- The sisters do not really trust each other, but they have to pretend to be in accord.

- Goneril wants Edmund and his boldness for her own, but she does not want to let Regan know this.

- She needs to advise Regan on what to do in terms of war and political conflict.

- All Goneril does and says is out of self-preservation and to further herself and her wealth. She is crafty and not above lying to get what she wants.

ACTIVITY 18
A Marriage Gone Bad

Act four, Scene 2

Background   When Albany comes home, he and Goneril have nothing but insults to trade with each other.

Directions   To better understand their dissatisfaction with each other, answer the following questions about Albany's and Goneril's lines. Use another sheet of paper, if necessary.

Albany: O Goneril!/You are not worth the dust which the rude wind/Blows in your face. I fear your disposition:/That nature, which contemns its origin,/Cannot be bordered certain in itself;/She that herself will sliver and disbranch/From her material sap, perforce must wither/And come to deadly use.

1. What does Albany mean about condemning her origin? How has Goneril turned her back on her origin, and how can that spell future disaster?

Albany: A father, and a gracious aged man,/Whose reverence even the head-lugged bear would lick,/Most barbarous, most degenerate, have you madded./Could my good brother suffer you to do it? A man, a prince, by him so benfited!/If that the heavens do not their visible spirits/Send quickly down to tame these vile offences,/It will come,/Humanity must perforce prey on itself,/Like monsters of the deep.

2. Whom has Goneril made insane?
3. What does Albany predict will happen if these offenses are not punished?
4. According to Albany, what exactly are these offenses?

Goneril: . . . That not know'st/Fools do those villains pity who are punished/Ere they have done their mischief./Where's they drum?/France spreads his banners in our noiseless land,/With plumed helm thy state begins to threat,/Whilst thou, a moral fool, sits still, and cries/'Alack! why does he so?'

5. According to Goneril, her father was a villain who was punished before he could do his mischief. What does this mean?
6. Why is Goneril angry with Albany concerning France?

ACTIVITY 19
The Letter Informing Cordelia of All Act four, Scene 3

Background Kent asks the Gentleman if the letters describing all that has happened since Cordelia was disowned by her father have moved her.

Directions Write the letter Kent was inquiring about, being sure to include all of the major events that have occurred since Cordelia left to marry the King of France. When finished, write a sentence or two about what kind of person you judge Cordelia to be based on her reaction to this letter, even after her father has banished her. Suggested length: ½ of a page to ¾ of a page. Use another sheet of paper, if necessary.

ACTIVITY 20

Review

Directions Read the following. Then write the letter of the correct answer in the space provided.

___ 1. Edgar, in disguise, calls himself
   a. Harry.
   b. Tom.
   c. Edgar.
   d. Edmund.

___ 2. Gloucester is trying to get to
   a. London.
   b. Bath.
   c. Dover.
   d. Goneril's house.

___ 3. With whom has Goneril formed an alliance?
   a. Edmund
   b. Kent
   c. Gloucester
   d. Edgar

___ 4. Whose death do we learn of in this act?
   a. Albany
   b. Cornwall
   c. King Lear
   d. Gloucester

___ 5. Goneril receives a letter from
   a. her husband.
   b. Edmund.
   c. Regan.
   d. Cordelia.

___ 6. Cordelia is now the Queen of
   a. Britain.
   b. Denmark.
   c. France.
   d. Italy.

___ 7. How does Cordelia find out about her father?
   a. She receives a letter.
   b. Kent visits her.
   c. Regan tells her.
   d. A carrier pigeon delivers the message.

(continued)

ACTIVITY 20

Review (continued)

Directions Match the character with his or her actions thus far. Write the letter of the correct action in the space provided.

Character   **Action**

___ 8. Kent   a. pretends to be an insane beggar

___ 9. King Lear   b. disguises himself to stay close to King Lear

___ 10. Cordelia   c. rebukes his wife for her evil ways

___ 11. Goneril   d. rages at his daughters amidst a terrible storm

___ 12. Albany   e. is blinded and thrust out into the night

___ 13. Gloucester   f. remains loyal to her father

___ 14. Edmund   g. thinks her husband is weak

___ 15. Edgar   h. betrays his family for personal gain

ACTIVITY 21
Nature of Man Questionnaire

Background Shakespeare has given us many different kinds of characters in this play, from those who are straightforward and honest to those who are deceitful and evil.

Directions To better understand the characters and themes presented in the play, answer the following questions as thoroughly and as thoughtfully as possible. You may be expected to share or discuss your answers in class. Use another sheet of paper on which to write your answers.

1. Few would argue that some people are just plain mean, or even evil. Do you think humans are *born* with a propensity toward good or evil, or are those inclinations gained only as we grow and experience the world? Explain.

2. Do you believe there are people in the world as evil as Edmund, Regan, or Goneril, who would betray anyone to get ahead? Why or why not?

3. Do you believe there are people as pure and good as Cordelia, who, even when wronged, think only of forgiveness and acts of love? Explain.

4. What message do you think Shakespeare was trying to send to his audience, and the world, in this play?

5. If you were in Cordelia's situation, do you think you could forgive your father? Why or why not?

6. Does King Lear, based on his actions early in the play, deserve the treatment he has received? Why or why not?

7. Do you believe in *karma*—that bad things will come to bad people and vice versa? Explain.

8. How would *you* like to see this play end?

ACTIVITY 22
A Portrait of Three Sisters

Act four, Scene 3

Background In Act four, Scene 3, Kent says the following when contemplating how different Cordelia is from her greedy, immoral sisters: "It is the stars,/The stars above us, govern our conditions;/Else one self mate and make could not beget/Such different issues." Kent is saying that it is hard to believe Goneril, Regan, and Cordelia are so different, yet they come from the same father.

Directions Imagine Goneril, Regan, and Cordelia as little girls, and create a "flashback" scene for the play that illustrates their different natures, even back then. Write it in modern verse and in play format. Suggested length: 2 pages, or approximately 50 lines. Use another sheet of paper.

ACTIVITY 23
Wisdom in Insanity

Act four, Scene 6

Background After Edgar convinces his father (who does not yet recognize his son) that he is meant to live and not take his own life, King Lear stumbles in wearing wild flowers and talking insanely. Amid Lear's mad ramblings, Edgar comments: "O, matter and impertinency mixed; reason in madness," meaning that Lear is mumbling truth along with nonsense.

Directions Come up with at least four truths that Lear expresses in this scene. Write the line, and then explain the truth inherent within it.

ACTIVITY 24
Headlining

Act four

Background Much of the important action in *King Lear* occurs in Act four as the play builds up to its tragic conclusion.

Directions Decide which event is most important to each of the scenes in Act four. Then write a headline depicting those events for each of the seven scenes. Remember: Headlines often employ alliteration ("**B**rawny **B**adgers **B**ludgeon Eagles in Semifinals"), use vivid action verbs, and are straightforward and attention-getting. Generally, articles (a, an, the) are left out of headlines.

1. Scene 1 Headline:

2. Scene 2 Headline:

3. Scene 3 Headline:

4. Scene 4 Headline:

5. Scene 5 Headline:

6. Scene 6 Headline:

7. Scene 7 Headline:

ACTIVITY 25
Review

Directions   Number the following events from the first four acts of *King Lear* to match the order in which they occurred.

Act one   ___ Edmund tells Gloucester that Edgar is plotting against him.

___ Goneril demands that King Lear reduce his retinue.

___ Kent disguises himself as a servant to stay near to King Lear.

___ Cordelia is disowned.

Act two   ___ King Lear angrily leaves and goes off into the stormy night.

___ Edgar decides to disguise himself as a mad beggar.

___ Edmund stages a pretend fight with Edgar.

___ Kent picks a fight with Oswald.

Act three   ___ Gloucester is blinded.

___ Gloucester confides in his son, Edmund, who then betrays him.

___ Kent gives the Gentleman a ring and a letter to carry to Cordelia.

___ Cornwall is wounded by a servant trying to protect Gloucester.

Act four   ___ Gloucester and Edgar are reunited (although Gloucester does not realize it).

___ Gloucester thinks he has jumped off a cliff but is spared from death.

___ Cordelia has a doctor treat her father, and she and her father speak.

___ Edmund and Goneril kiss and form an alliance.

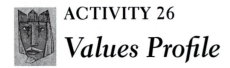

ACTIVITY 26
Values Profile

Background By Act five, Scene 1, it seems that Edmund, Goneril, and Regan could not sink any lower into their deplorable, self-serving behavior. Albany, by contrast, is openly regretful about opposing King Lear and Cordelia's husband (the King of France), but he must protect his land and property.

Directions Consider the following characters and what they value most and least, based on their words and actions throughout the play. Rate all characters, but then choose two characters and explain your value ratings for those two in depth, using dialogue or events from the play for explanation and support of your choices. Rankings go from 1 as most important to 6 as least important. Use another sheet of paper for your two character assessments.

Goneril
____ Love
____ Integrity
____ Power
____ Honor
____ Wealth
____ Honesty

Albany
____ Love
____ Integrity
____ Power
____ Honor
____ Wealth
____ Honesty

Edmund
____ Love
____ Integrity
____ Power
____ Honor
____ Wealth
____ Honesty

Cordelia
____ Love
____ Integrity
____ Power
____ Honor
____ Wealth
____ Honesty

King Lear
____ Love
____ Integrity
____ Power
____ Honor
____ Wealth
____ Honesty

Kent
____ Love
____ Integrity
____ Power
____ Honor
____ Wealth
____ Honesty

ACTIVITY 27
Spying on Edmund

Act five, Scene 1

Background   At the end of Scene 1, Edmund's speech reveals much about his intentions toward Goneril, Regan, and Albany, as well as his plans for Lear and Cordelia, should he win the war against France.

Directions   Edgar has recently been speaking (in disguise) to Albany. Imagine you are Edgar, eavesdropping on Edmund, who is right around the corner. You are collecting mounting evidence of Edgar's treachery, and you will be writing down his evil intentions to later present to Albany or the King of France. Suggested Length: ½ of a page to ¾ of a page. Use another sheet of paper, if necessary.

ACTIVITY 28
Reviewing the Deaths

Background As in most Shakespearean tragedies, many of the characters have died by the end of the play.

Directions To check your understanding and recall of events in the play, briefly explain how the following characters died and find the line that mentions each character's death.

Cornwall:

Oswald:

Gloucester:

Regan:

Goneril:

Edmund:

Cordelia:

King Lear:

ACTIVITY 29
Writing an Obituary

Background An obituary is a written remembrance of a person after he or she has died, mentioning his or her accomplishments in life, surviving family members, information about the funeral, and so forth.

Directions Write an obituary about King Lear, Gloucester, or Cordelia. Make sure that what you write reflects what you know of the character based on the lines and events in the play. Think carefully about how you will word the obituary, as it needs to appropriately portray and pay tribute to the deceased. You may want to check the newspaper to get a better sense of what an obituary looks like and contains.

ACTIVITY 30
Review

Directions Read the following quotations from *King Lear,* and, in the space provided, write the letter of the character who spoke the line.

___ 1. "Unhappy that I am, I cannot heave my heart into my mouth: I love your Majesty according to my bond; no more nor less."
   a. Regan   c. Cordelia
   b. Goneril   d. Gloucester

___ 2. "Fare thee well, King; sith thus thou wilt appear, Freedom lives hence, and banishment is here."
   a. Kent   c. Gloucester
   b. Albany   d. Cornwall

___ 3. "Fairest Cordelia, that art most rich, being poor; most choice, forsaken; and most loved, despised! Thee and thy virtues here I seize upon: Be it lawful I take up what's cast away."
   a. Cornwall   c. Kent
   b. Burgundy   d. France

___ 4. "Time shall unfold what plighted cunning hides; who cover faults, at last shame them derides. Well may you prosper!"
   a. Cordelia   c. Goneril
   b. Kent   d. Regan

___ 5. "For that I am some twelve or fourteen moonshines lag of a brother? Why bastard? Wherefore base?"
   a. Edmund   c. Kent
   b. Edgar   d. Gloucester

___ 6. "His knights grow riotous, and himself upbraids us on every trifle."
   a. Oswald   c. Goneril
   b. Regan   d. Cornwall

___ 7. "If thou canst serve where thou dost stand condemned, so may it come, thy master, whom thou lovest, shall find thee full of labours."
   a. King Lear   c. Fool
   b. Edgar   d. Kent

___ 8. "Sir, I am too old to learn. Call not your stocks for me; I serve the King, on whose employment I was sent to you; you shall do small respect, show too bold malice against the grace and person of my master, stocking his messenger."
   a. Kent   c. Cornwall
   b. Oswald   d. King Lear

___ 9. "I have received a hurt. Follow me, lady. Turn out that eyeless villain; throw this slave upon the dunghill."
   a. Gloucester   c. Cornwall
   b. Regan   d. Albany

___ 10. "I have sworn my love to both these sisters."
   a. Edgar   c. Cornwall
   b. Edmund   d. Albany

© 2004 Walch Publishing   32   *Shakespeare Made Easy: King Lear*

King Lear

Final Test

Directions: Read each statement. Then write true (T) or false (F) in the space provided.

___ 1. The last person to die in the play is Cordelia.

___ 2. The King of France is forced to take Cordelia as his wife.

___ 3. Goneril is the eldest daughter.

___ 4. King Lear feels his one hundred knight retinue is necessary.

___ 5. Edgar writes a fake letter that implicates Edmund in a betrayal of their father.

___ 6. Albany tries to reason with King Lear after King Lear disinherits Cordelia.

___ 7. Burgundy rejects Cordelia after her dowry is taken away.

___ 8. Oswald is Goneril's steward.

___ 9. Gloucester believes he has been spared from death after being convinced he survived a leap off of a cliff.

___ 10. King Lear is murdered.

Directions: Choose the letter of the best answer. Write it in the space provided.

___ 11. Who slays Oswald?
  a. Edgar
  b. Edmund
  c. Kent
  d. King Lear

___ 12. Who writes Edgar a letter asking for the death of her husband?
  a. Regan
  b. Goneril
  c. Cordelia
  d. the Queen of France

___ 13. Who gets poisoned?
  a. Regan
  b. Goneril
  c. King Lear
  d. Gloucester

___ 14. Which two countries go to war?
  a. Britain and Germany
  b. Italy and France
  c. France and Britain
  d. Britain and Denmark

(continued)

King Lear   **Final Test** *(continued)*

___ 15. Who kills herself?
    a. Regan
    b. Goneril
    c. Cordelia
    d. the Queen of France

___ 16. Why does Lear want his daughters to express their love for him in the first act?
    a. so that his royal court hears how much he is beloved
    b. so that he may decide how to divide his kingdom
    c. so that he may decide which daughter he will marry to the King of France
    d. none of the above

___ 17. Why does Cordelia not express her love in the same way her sisters do?
    a. She does not love her father as much as they do.
    b. She is angry at her sisters and unwilling to speak.
    c. Although she loves her father deeply, she is unable to embellish or articulate her love.
    d. both a and b

___ 18. Why is Edmund so angry and vengeful?
    a. He feels wronged by his illegitimate birth and subsequent treatment as an inferior.
    b. He hates King Lear and wants to control Britain.
    c. His brother Edgar has betrayed him before.
    d. none of the above

___ 19. Why are Regan and Goneril so eager to form an alliance with Edmund?
    a. They think he will be the next ruler of Britain.
    b. They think he is the only person they can trust.
    c. Edmund has promised that they will be co-rulers of Britain and France.
    d. Both of their husbands have betrayed them, and they are vulnerable.

___ 20. Why is Kent put in the stocks?
    a. for protecting Gloucester
    b. for defending Cordelia
    c. for disagreeing with Albany
    d. for assaulting Oswald

CULMINATING ACTIVITY 1
Nature and the Nature of Man

Directions Throughout *King Lear,* Shakespeare's characters comment on nature in two senses: mother nature and the nature of man. Many of the characters comment on the nature of man and the depravity of man. Write a multi-paragraph essay analyzing the themes of this dual concept of nature and what Shakespeare was trying to say through it all. Use quotations and events from the play for support. Suggested length: 3–5 pages. Use additional sheets of paper.

CULMINATING ACTIVITY 2
Create a Movie Poster or a Book Jacket

Directions Imagine that you are a graphic designer working on designing either a movie poster or a book jacket to promote *King Lear*. Incorporate one of the major events from the play and as many of the characters as possible into your design. Make the design enticing and colorful, so that anyone seeing it would feel compelled to read the book or see the movie. Make both the lettering and design big and easy to read. You may use poster board or another sheet of paper for your design.

CULMINATING ACTIVITY 3
King Lear *and* Current Events

Directions Choose a line or quotation (must be a complete thought) from the play and attach it to a modern-day event to demonstrate that, despite being written long ago, Shakespeare's words still carry relevance today. Print the quotation or line in large, easy-to-read letters on poster board along with the modern-day event (occurring within the last five years), which should be drawn or shown in a collage. On the back, write a brief explanation of how the quotation relates to the event.

CULMINATING ACTIVITY 4
Put It to Music

Directions   Students should work in groups of no more than four for this activity, and one student in each group must have access to a CD burner. Choose one or two events that are central to each act (no more than 10 songs total), and find a song that fits the mood of each event. Create a CD, including a cover that is suited to *King Lear*. On the back, list all of the song titles, the events the songs are representing, and the genre of each song (rock, country, jazz, and so forth). The songs may fit the event either because of the title, lyrics, or overall mood of the music.

CULMINATING ACTIVITY 5
Write Your Own Ending

Directions Shakespeare certainly avoids a happy ending in this play, with the French army defeated by the British and Lear, Cordelia, and Gloucester all dying. Consider how you would like to see this play end, and write a new ending for it. Suggested length: 4–8 typewritten, double-spaced pages in play format.

King Lear

Answer Key

Activity 1
Answers will vary.

Activity 2
Answers will vary, but the following may serve as a guide:

King of France: Perhaps he is marrying Cordelia because he wants an inside track on how to infiltrate Britain's power so that he may win in war.

Edmund: He is planning to make his brother look bad so that he may gain more power, prestige, and inheritance.

Goneril and Regan: They are both plotting to strip their father of his power and rule Britain.

Kent: He is planning to disguise himself as a servant to Lear so that he may get back into Lear's good graces.

Activity 3
Answers will vary.

Activity 4
1. King Lear has alienated two of his daughters and blessed the third one unknowingly (Cordelia, by getting her away from him). If you really want to follow someone who is so backward and full of error, then you should wear my jester's cap.
2. Give up drinking and sleeping with prostitutes and stay inside, and you will have more than you have now (because you keep giving everything away).
3. Whoever helped you to decide to give away your land, ask him to come and represent me, and then you pretend to be him. We have traded places (you as the Fool because you have made such dumb choices lately).
4. When you gave your lands and power to Goneril and Regan, you were like the man in the fable who carried the donkey on his back over the mud (instead of the other way around). You weren't in your right mind (or your bald head!) when you made such a foolish decision.

Activity 5
1. c
2. b
3. c
4. b
5. b
6. b
7. b
8. T
9. a
10. c

Activity 6
Answers will vary.

Activity 7
Answers will vary.

Activity 8
Answers will vary, but the following may serve as a guide:

1. He is saying that the difference between man and beast is our ability (even right) to desire that which we do not need, such as Lear "needs" his retinue of one hundred men.
2. Lear says that his daughters don't need their gorgeous clothes and jewelry, but it

King Lear — Answer Key

makes them feel worthy even when it is impractical. It's the same for Lear; his self-esteem is tied up in his material possessions and his many knights.

3–5. Answers will vary.

Activity 9
Answers will vary.

Activity 10
1. f
2. b
3. a
4. e
5. h
6. d
7. c
8. g
9. i
10. j

Activity 11
Answers may vary slightly.

1. "There is division, although as yet the face of it is covered with mutual cunning, 'twixt Albany and Cornwall. . . ."
2. a. the quarrels of the Dukes
   b. how they have dealt with Lear
   c. something more important and more significant than the other two things
3. France is prepared to reveal itself and start warring.
4. Kent wants Cordelia to know the information in the letter is true and accurate (and that it's from him).
5. King Lear

Activity 12
Answers will vary.

Activity 13
Answers will vary, but the following may serve as a guide:

When we see our superiors suffering, our private woes seem insignificant. Whoever suffers alone, suffers most anguish mentally, discarding unimportant and trifling concerns. But then the mind is relieved when there are others to share in the suffering because it makes it more bearable. How insignificant my pain seems now when the King is suffering so cruelly. He suffers from his children, and I from my father. I need to move cautiously and consider all of the rumors of what's going on. I will reveal myself when I have cleared my name and reconciled to my father. Whatever happens tonight, I hope King Lear escapes safely. Meanwhile, I will stay in hiding.

Activity 14
Answers will vary, but the following may serve as a guide:

Event 1: King Lear is going insane and ranting and raving during the storm.

Significance: His daughters' treatment of him and his guilt over wronging Cordelia have pushed him over the edge mentally and emotionally.

Event 2: The King will be avenged of the wrongs done to him by his daughters.

Significance: France is planning to wage war to avenge him.

Event 3: I (Edmund) will betray my father and tell of France's intent so that he is punished and I am praised. I will rise to power as he falls to poverty.

King Lear — Answer Key

Significance: Edmund is going to betray his father.

Event 4: Gloucester will be blinded.

Significance: He is considered a traitor and will be thrown out. This event also makes clear the extremely cruel natures of Goneril and Regan.

Event 5: Cornwall is wounded in a scuffle (a servant rushes to Gloucester's defense).

Significance: Cornwall may die from his wounds.

Activity 15

1. T
2. T
3. F
4. T
5. T
6. F
7. F
8. T
9. F
10. F

Activity 16
Scenes will vary.

Activity 17
Letters will vary.

Activity 18
Answers will vary, but the following may serve as a guide:

1. By abandoning her father and allowing him to wander in the storm, she is rejecting where she came from. According to Shakespearean "law," no good comes to those who practice evil: Goneril will be punished for this some way, somehow.
2. Goneril has contributed to her father's insanity.
3. If the offenses are not punished, humanity will just get worse and more evil and become cannibalistic, each human looking out for only himself or herself.
4. Goneril has treated her father with complete disrespect and hatred.
5. If Lear had been allowed to keep his one hundred men and his lands and titles, he would have done much mischief and evil, so Goneril paints herself as one who has saved everyone from this supposedly evil King.
6. She thinks that he is a coward; France is ready to go to war, and Albany sits there preaching to her instead of taking any military action against France.

Activity 19
Letters and responses will vary.

Activity 20

1. b
2. c
3. a
4. b
5. c
6. c
7. a
8. b
9. d
10. f
11. g
12. c
13. e
14. h
15. a

Activity 21
Answers will vary.

Activity 22
Scenes will vary.

King Lear — Answer Key

Activity 23

Answers will vary.

1. "When the rain came to wet me once and the wind to make me chatter . . . there I found 'em, there I smelt 'em out." They (Goneril and Regan) flattered and fawned upon me and made me believe I was invincible, but here I am shivering in this storm. It was all lies. Lear is realizing that Goneril and Regan have never loved him, and his life has amounted to ranting in a storm.

2. "A man may see how this world goes/with no eyes." A man doesn't need to see to understand the ways of the world. All is disappointment and betrayal, so why bother seeing or trying?

3. "A dog's obeyed in office." Even a dog is obeyed when it has a title. Had I kept my lands, I would not be in this mess. Power and possession make a man invincible.

4. "Thou rascal beadle, hold thy bloody hand!/Why dost thou lash that whore? Strip thine own back;/Thou hotly lusts to use her in that kind/For which thou whip'st her." Strip the skin off your own back; you want the very thing you are punishing her for. We are all sinners; it's just a matter of degrees.

Activity 24

Headlines will vary.

Activity 25

Order of events:

    Act one: 2, 4, 3, 1

    Act two: 3, 4, 1, 2

    Act three: 3, 2, 1, 4

    Act four: 1, 4, 3, 2

Activity 26

Answers will vary.

Activity 27

Answers will vary, but the following may serve as a guide:

Edgar has made alliances with both sisters, but he cannot decide which to take. Neither is any good to him if they both remain alive. To take Regan would infuriate Goneril, but he cannot have Goneril if Albany remains alive. So, he will use Albany as a military pawn and then plan his death with Goneril later. Albany plans to let Cordelia and Lear live after the war, but Edmund wants them dead. He needs to act rather than think.

Activity 28

Cornwall dies from wounds suffered from a servant who protects Gloucester: "O my good Lord, the Duke of Cornwell's dead; slain by his servant, going to put out the other eye of Gloucester."

Oswald dies after he and Edgar fight, and Edgar slays him: "Slave, thou hast slain me."

Gloucester dies of a heart attack after Edgar tells him the truth about Edmund and all that has occurred: ". . . but his flawed heart, alack, too weak the conflict to support, 'twixt two extremes of passion, joy and grief, burst smilingly."

Regan dies from poison that her sister, Goneril, gives her: "Your lady, sir, your lady: and her sister [Regan] by her is poisoned. . . ."

King Lear — Answer Key

Goneril stabs herself: "'Tis hot, it smokes; it came even from the heart of—O, she's dead!"

Edmund dies after receiving a fatal wound from fighting Edgar: "Edmund is dead, my lord."

Cordelia dies by hanging (on orders of Edmund): "She's dead as earth."

Lear dies after holding the dead Cordelia in his arms: "He is gone indeed."

Activity 29
Obituaries will vary.

Activity 30
1. c
2. a
3. d
4. a
5. a
6. c
7. d
8. a
9. c
10. b

Final Test Answers
1. F
2. F
3. T
4. T
5. F
6. F
7. T
8. T
9. T
10. F
11. a
12. b
13. a
14. c
15. b
16. b
17. c
18. a
19. a
20. d

Culminating Activity 1
Essays will vary, but the following may serve as grading guidelines:

- Strong thesis that remained the focus for entire paper
- Textual support
- Within length guidelines
- Properly attributed quotations from play
- Demonstrated understanding of text
- Well-supported thesis
- Proper spelling and punctuation

Culminating Activity 2
Posters and book jackets will vary. Here are some possible grading guidelines:

- Colorful
- Easy to read
- Incorporated title
- Represented the book and events appropriately

Culminating Activity 3
Responses will vary, but the following may serve as a grading guideline:

- Event from text is correctly interpreted.
- Pictures, illustrations, and words are clearly visible.
- Parallel to modern-day event makes sense and shows insight into text.

Culminating Activity 4
CDs and covers will vary.

Culminating Activity 5
Responses will vary, but the following may serve as a grading guideline:

- Response followed length guideline and is typed and double-spaced.
- The ending is in keeping with the tone of the original text (not unrealistic).

Share Your Bright Ideas

We want to hear from you!

Your name_____Date_____

School name_____

School address_____

City _____State_____Zip_____Phone number (_____)_____

Grade level(s) taught_____Subject area(s) taught_____

Where did you purchase this publication?_____

In what month do you purchase a majority of your supplements?_____

What moneys were used to purchase this product?

___School supplemental budget   ___Federal/state funding   ___Personal

Please "grade" this Walch publication in the following areas:

Quality of service you received when purchasing .... A B C D
Ease of use .... A B C D
Quality of content .... A B C D
Page layout .... A B C D
Organization of material .... A B C D
Suitability for grade level .... A B C D
Instructional value .... A B C D

COMMENTS:_____

_____

What specific supplemental materials would help you meet your current—or future—instructional needs?

_____

Have you used other Walch publications? If so, which ones?_____

May we use your comments in upcoming communications?   ___Yes   ___No

Please **FAX** this completed form to **888-991-5755**, or mail it to

Customer Service, Walch Publishing, P. O. Box 658, Portland, ME 04104-0658

We will send you a **FREE GIFT** in appreciation of your feedback. **THANK YOU!**